Extreme Halfpipe Snowboarding Moves

By Mary Firestone

Consultant:
Jennifer Sherowski
Senior Editor
TransWorld SNOWboarding Magazine

CAPSTONE
HIGH-INTEREST
BOOKS

an imprint of Capstone Press
Mankato, Minnesota

Capstone High-Interest Books are published by Capstone Press
151 Good Counsel Drive, P.O. Box 669, Mankato, Minnesota 56002
http://www.capstone-press.com

Library of Congress Cataloging-in-Publication Data
Firestone, Mary.
   Extreme halfpipe snowboarding moves / by Mary Firestone.
   p. cm.—(Behind the moves)
   Summary: Discusses the elements of the sport of snowboarding that take
it to the extreme in snowy halfpipes. Includes bibliographical references and index.
   ISBN 0-7368-2154-6
   1. Snowboarding—Juvenile literature. 2. Extreme sports—Juvenile literature.
[1. Snowboarding. 2. Extreme sports.] I. Title. II. Series.
GV857.S57F57 2004
796.9—dc21   2002156470

Editorial Credits
James Anderson, editor; Jason Knudson, book designer; Jo Miller, photo
   researcher; Karen Risch, product planning editor

Photo Credits
Corbis/Reuters NewMedia, Inc., 4, 16; Duomo, 8, 10
Getty Images, 29; Donald Miralle, 25; Zoom Sports, 13
Jennifer Sherowski, 22
PhotoDisc Inc., 4 (inset), 10 (inset), 18 (inset), 26 (inset)
SportsChrome-USA, cover, 7, 15, 21, 24, 26; Rob Tringali, 14, 18

Table of Contents

Learn about:

- **Modern snowboards**
- **Early halfpipes**
- **Board shapes**

Chapter One

Halfpipe Snowboarding

Snowboarder Ross Powers had fallen hard in his first qualifying run for the halfpipe competition at the 2002 Winter Olympics in Salt Lake City, Utah. He needed a good score in the finals to win the gold medal.

Powers pushed quickly off the ledge. He went up the pipe wall, high into the bright, sunny sky. His first trick was a backside air. He then went to a frontside air. He moved to a McTwist, then a frontside 720 with an Indy grab. Powers finished with another 720 Indy grab, then a stalefish to a backside 360 mute, followed by a switch McTwist.

Powers won the Olympic gold medal. He stomped each trick. It was the most successful run of his career.

Modern Snowboards

In the 1960s, a man from Vermont named Jake Burton Carpenter competed in early downhill snowboard races. He later designed his own snowboards. Carpenter learned as much as he could about snowboarding. He tried different board shapes until he found what worked best.

Carpenter's boards had bindings, which earlier boards did not have. Bindings attach a rider's boots to the snowboard. Bindings made it easier for more people to ride snowboards. Other companies quickly made similar designs.

Halfpipe History

Halfpipe snowboarding began in the 1970s when skateboarders and surfers learned to snowboard. They brought their love for extreme riding to the mountains.

In the early days of snowboarding, riders searched for creek beds and drainage ditches. They shoveled and shaped the snow to smooth the walls of these natural halfpipes.

When snowboarding became popular in the 1980s, ski areas built halfpipes. Today, many ski areas have superpipes like the one used in the 2002 Winter Olympics. Superpipe walls are 15 to 17 feet (4 to 5 meters) high. The superpipe's high walls help riders get more air on their jumps.

Bindings hold a rider's boots to the board.

Halfpipe riders use a freestyle board.

Freestyle Boards

Today, snowboards are made of foam, wood, fiberglass, and carbon fiber. Some boards are specially designed for downhill, freestyle, or powder snow riding. Each board has a different shape.

Halfpipe riders prefer the freestyle board. Freestyle boards have a twin tip shape. Both the tail and nose of the freestyle board are nearly the same distance from the bindings. A freestyle board's tips are turned upward. The upward curves match the curves of a halfpipe.

Snowboards are measured in centimeters. They are usually between 100 and 180 centimeters (39 and 71 inches) long. Most snowboards are 15 to 30 centimeters (6 to 12 inches) wide.

Bindings are attached to the board in either regular or goofy foot position. Many riders prefer snowboarding with their left foot forward, which is called riding regular. Some riders are more comfortable with their right foot in front. This is called goofy foot.

Most tricks are done above the halfpipe.

Learn about:

☐ **Dropping in**

☐ **Getting out**

☐ **Big air**

Chapter Two

Basic Moves

Before trying the halfpipe, snowboarders should be good at turning their boards on the ski slopes. Beginner ski runs are the best place for riders to learn how to snowboard.

Riding the Walls

Snowboarders first practice on halfpipes by riding the walls. They ride into the pipe from the top of either wall. This is called dropping in. The momentum, or speed, from dropping in pulls riders forward across the pipe. Riders then go to the frontside or backside wall.

The frontside wall is in the direction a rider's toes face. The backside is in the direction that a rider's heels face. Either wall can be the frontside or backside wall, depending on which way a rider is moving.

Snowboarders gain speed on the transition, or center of the halfpipe. They bend their knees and push down with their feet. Snowboarders call this "pumping," or "pumping the tranny."

Getting Out

After snowboarders learn basic moves inside the pipe, they focus on getting out. The rider's body and snowboard rise above the walls of the pipe into the air. The rider returns to the halfpipe without falling. Once riders master getting out, they are skilled enough to try more difficult tricks.

Riders get air by doing an ollie at the top of the pipe. To do an ollie, riders push on the board with their back foot, forcing the board into the air.

Riders practice inside the pipe before getting out.

13

Grabs

During a grab, a snowboarder grabs onto a part of their board. Some basic grabs are the mute, Indy, method, and tail grab.

To do a mute grab, a rider grabs the toe edge with the front hand. An Indy grab is also grabbing the toe edge, but with the rear hand instead of the front hand. A rider grabs the heel side of the board during a method grab. For nose or tail grabs, the rider grabs the nose with the front hand, or the tail with the rear hand.

Method grabs are common moves.

Straight Airs

When riders jump high, they get big air. When riders get comfortable getting out of the halfpipe, they try straight airs.

A straight air is a 180-degree spin added to a jump. A 180-degree spin is a half turn. This spin is done in the air above the pipe.

As riders become skilled at the pipe, they try alley-oops and 360 spins. An alley-oop is a 180-degree spin toward the top of the pipe. A 360-degree spin is a full spin landing fakie. A fakie landing is to land riding backward.

Snowboarders add more difficult spins and grabs to straight airs as they get better. This is one way that new tricks are invented.

Straight air

15

Halfpipe Snowboarding Slang

bail—to fall

goofy foot—to ride with the right foot in front; regular position is with the left foot in front.

ill—cool, good

invert—to turn upside down

jib—snowboarding on something other than snow, such as trees or handrails

jibbers—another name for freestyle snowboarders

ollie—shifting weight to the back of the board, which builds energy to lift the board

rolling down the windows—when riders frantically wave their arms in the air as they are about to crash

stomp—to land after a trick without putting a hand on the ground

Inverts are tricks done upside down.

Learn about:

- Difficult grabs
- The McTwist
- Combinations

Chapter Three

Extreme Moves

Skilled riders perform tricks above the pipe. They do inverts, spins, and grabs. These riders get big air.

Moves above the Pipe

Expert riders reach heights of 15 to 20 feet (5 to 6 meters) above the edge of the pipe. Riders need big air to have more time to hold a grab or perform a trick.

Moves performed upside down are called inverts. To do an invert, riders jump into the air and turn a half somersault. They remain in the upside-down position while doing spins and grabs.

Grabs are often combined with big air moves. A rider's weight shifts during a grab. Grabs are sometimes used during a big air move to change the direction of a spin.

There is a name for almost every way to grab a board. Grabbing the heel edge while leaning over the nose is called a lien air. A melancholie air is grabbing the heel side of the board with the front hand. A rocket air is grabbing the nose of the board and pulling back. To do a truck driver, a rider grabs between the bindings with both hands. For a roast beef grab, the rider places the rear hand between the bindings and grabs the heel edge while straightening the front leg.

A truck driver is a grab with both hands.

Multiple Moves

Riders combine several basic moves into a single trick once they are good enough at basic tricks. Some multiple moves have become as common as basic tricks. The McTwist, rodeo flip, misty flip, and eggplant are some of these tricks.

The McTwist combines an inverted mute grab with a frontflip and a 540. A 540 is a full turn plus a half turn. Riders often add other grabs to the McTwist. The rodeo flip is an inverted frontside 540. A misty flip is a 540 rotation combined with a back flip. An eggplant starts with a 180 inverted backside. Then, the front hand is planted on the edge of the halfpipe.

Snowboarders try to land high inside the halfpipe when they do multiple tricks. Landing high helps maintain speed for the next hit. A hit is a run at the edge of the pipe. During each hit, a snowboarder has a chance to try more moves.

Combinations

The most difficult moves in halfpipe snowboarding were invented when riders put several multiple moves together into one hit. These moves are called combinations. Most combination moves are now considered single moves. The switch McTwist 900 and the crippler are just two of these moves.

The switch McTwist 900 is an inverted McTwist with an extra 360 spin added. A switch is done when either the takeoff or the landing is fakie.

During a crippler, riders rotate 90 degrees while doing a flip in the air. Riders then rotate another 90 degrees before they land.

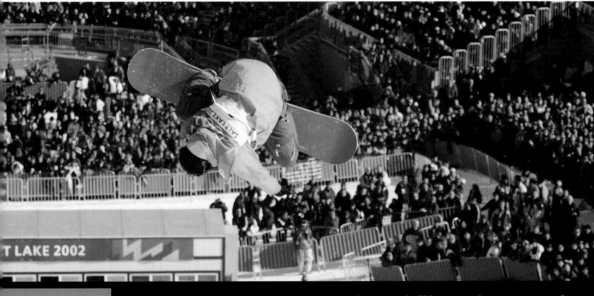

During a crippler, riders spin and flip at the same time.

A switch McTwist 900 includes two and one-half turns.

Snowboarders risk falling when they get air.

Learn about:

- Equipment
- Clothing
- Hypothermia

Chapter Four

Safety

Snowboarders get big air during some moves. They also go as fast as 30 miles (48 kilometers) per hour. Falling during these moves can cause serious injuries. Today's snowboarding equipment is designed to help prevent injuries.

Gear

Proper gear and clothing can help keep snowboarders safe. Some riders wear pants with padding built into the seat and knees. Competition riders wear helmets and wrist pads. Snowboarders wear goggles to protect their eyes from the sun. They also wear sunscreen to protect against sunburn.

Dressing in layers keeps snowboarders warm on cold days. Riders can remove or add layers of clothing if they become too hot or cold. The outer layer of clothing should be waterproof.

If riders are not dressed properly, they can get hypothermia. This condition occurs in people whose body temperature drops below 95 degrees Fahrenheit (35 degrees Celsius). People who have hypothermia can become confused and sleepy. If they are not careful, they may even die.

Fluids

Snowboarders should drink plenty of fluids. Drinking water or sports drinks gives the body the fluids it needs to function properly.

Snowboarders sweat during a run, and the sun dries their skin. This causes loss of fluids. Riders should drink 1 quart (1 liter) of water or sports drink for every hour they are snowboarding.

Halfpipe Safety

Snowboarders begin their runs by shouting, "dropping in." This lets riders know that someone is entering the halfpipe. Riders should take turns in the halfpipe and leave enough room in between to avoid crashes.

Respect for one another helps to keep the sport safe for all riders. Good safety habits allow snowboarders to keep inventing new moves.

Taking turns is a must in a halfpipe.

Words to Know

bindings (BINE-dings)—straps that hold a rider's feet to the snowboard

carbon fiber (KAR-buhn FYE-bur)—a strong, lightweight material used to make snowboards

hypothermia (hye-puh-THUR-mee-uh)—a condition that can occur when a person's body temperature falls several degrees below normal

momentum (moh-MEN-tuhm)—the force or speed a snowboarder has when moving

rotation (roh-TAY-shuhn)—a trick in which snowboarders spin at least 360 degrees in the air

superpipe (SOO-pur-pipe)—a halfpipe with walls higher than a normal halfpipe; superpipes are often used at professional competitions.

To Learn More

Fraser, Andy. *Snowboarding.* Radical Sports. Chicago: Heinemann Library, 2000.

Tomlinson, Joe. *Extreme Sports: The Illustrated Guide to Maximum Adrenaline Thrills.* New York: Carlton, 2002.

Young, Ian. *X Games: Action Sports Grab the Spotlight.* High Five Reading. Mankato, Minn.: Capstone Curriculim Publishing, 2003

Useful Addresses

Canadian Snowboard Federation
155 Canada Olympic Road SW
Calgary, AB T3B 5R5
Canada

United States of America Snowboard Association
P. O. Box 3927
Truckee, CA 96160

United States Ski and Snowboard Association
P. O. Box 100
1500 Kearns Boulevard
Building F
Park City, UT 84060

Internet Sites

Do you want to find out more about halfpipe snowboarding?
Let FactHound, our fact-finding hound dog, do the research for you.

Here's how:

1) Visit *http://www.facthound.com*
2) Type in the **Book ID** number: **0736821546**
3) Click on **FETCH IT**.

FactHound will fetch Internet sites picked by our editors just for you!

Index